Mind Over Money

How to Think Like An Investor and Take Care of Business First

Ryan McCrary

DEDICATION

Dedicated to everyone who inspires to do great things in the face of adversity.

CONTENTS

ACKNOWLEDGMENTS

This book would not have been possible without the support of my dear mother, Susan McCrary, my sister, Jessica McCrary, my grandmother, Carmen Lewis, and my aunt, Kathi Lewis.

To my children: Mariah and Logan, your future is what drives my ambition.

Also, a special thank you to the rest of my family, my friends, clients, students, and supporters. I sincerely appreciate all of your support.

Ryan McCrary

CHAPTER 1 – THE FINANCIALLY ILLITERATE AMERICAN

Close your eyes and think back to when you grew up and first started school. What is your first memory of school? Can you remember your very first day? Perhaps your first day of school was in kindergarten or first grade, or even pre-K. Maybe now you practice those same annual back to school routines with your children. Most of us can probably vividly remember those times, including how the weather was starting to change and how that cold fall air was right around the corner. At least that's how I remember my first day of school growing up on the East coast.

We would prepare with the right books, folders, pens, crayons, binders, erasers, etc. We would write each subject on each folder such as Math, English, Social Studies, or Science. These were the subjects that were the "most important" ones and every child *had* to learn these in order to be "smart".

Fast forward to high school—now you are taking more advanced subjects such as Trigonometry or Physics. You may even remember all of the sports or extra-curricular activities you joined in order to make your college application "look good" when you were applying to schools. As I reflect back, a question comes to mind: Why did we not ever learn the REAL information that would help us be successful in a capitalist society?

If you're reading this and you grew up in a society outside of the United States (which I hope is the case for some readers considering I would like to have an international impact), please bear with me as I explain the ridiculousness of growing up in an American capitalist society and never once being *required* to learn the information that impacts one's everyday life. Science is nice, and it is wonderful to learn about all of the different atoms and things that make up the world, but what good is organic chemistry jargon, if you are struggling to pay your rent on the 1st of every month? Does this make sense? I thought it would.

Before we move on, let's just outline the facts about the reality of capitalism in America. America is a business. Corporate America *is* America and America *is* corporate. I do truly believe that money is not everything, but in America it almost is. If you have no money then where will you live? How will you eat? Will the grocery store or local restaurant not want you to pay for food? Will they accept civil rights or social issues as a means of payment?

What about education? Luckily, we now have Google and education can actually be obtained for FREE, if you care to use your resources intentionally instead of using your smart phone for entertainment and when you recognize that you are holding a computer and potential multi-million-dollar business in your hand. However, when it pertains to the economics of education, why are the better schools the ones with more MONEY? What about healthcare? If you need to see a doctor or have to go to the hospital, if you have no MONEY for healthcare and no

MONEY to pay out of pocket, will you get seen? Yes, you will, but the facility will bill you. And if you get medical assistance and have less of a liability to pay as an individual, then the government is footing that bill, but trust and behold, it is not FREE.

These points are relevant ones that will ground our discussions in this book. This is not a political book on debating *if* America should change its ways and be "more like Europe" and other places that are more socialist or less capitalistic. We could debate all day about what *should* be done or what is right or wrong. No, I do not believe anybody in America should be homeless when there are 3 or 4 billionaires that hold more wealth than hundreds of millions of people but debating about it is not going to help us pay our bills or help our financial situation.

For this reason, it is important that we engage in a thoughtful dialogue about financial literacy and why many of us make the decisions that we do as it relates to our finances. One of the reasons why I understand how the world works from a sociological perspective is because I hold a Bachelor of Arts degree in sociology and have had far too many classes about Marx and socialism, globalization, inequalities, social injustice, etc. However, this book is not about those topics. While I loved my college experience, and learning at that level, 4 or 5 years of college still did not fully prepare me for the real world and it did not give me the financial knowledge I would need to face the financial challenges that exist in the *real world* especially being of the Millennial Generation. Ironically, most college degrees today won't even guarantee you a job.

The not-so-secret of the rich and wealthy (which there is a big difference between, which I will cover in later chapters) is the desire and *commitment* to incorporating financial literacy into their everyday lives. Now if you read carefully, you will see that I did not say *study* financial literacy; although I do believe *studying* financial literacy is extremely important—it is why I started an online Financial Literacy School in which you can sign up for free at www.themccraryfinancialschool.com. Commitment to financial literacy is not merely studying this information from a book or taking a $997 course from a social media influencer; it is about incorporating financial literacy into almost every aspect of how one lives one's life.

If the topics pertaining to financial literacy in this book sound like speaking a foreign language to you, guess what? This means that you are perfectly normal. I just want to stress to you that it is more than you just learning some concepts and telling yourself "you got to do better" and starting next year or next month, you will start "saving more money." It is about living your life in a completely different way than how you're currently accustomed.

Now this does not mean that you need to go out and completely transform who you are and become a complete miser. I am talking about MINDSET. You can do everything the same way as you are now, but with this new MINDSET, you will start to see that your ACTIONS will start following suit! Your MINDSET will adjust and then your ACTIONS will be different, not vice versa. Many people think that if I perform this ACTION then it will positively affect my MINDSET. This is true, but only temporarily. This book is about permanent changes that will enhance the financial health of your life.

For example, do you ever find yourself thinking: "If I take this lavish vacation that I really can't afford. . ." or "I go to this fancy restaurant. . ." just to take nice pictures on Instagram to appear to be "winning" because I am dining with the rich, that you will *feel* better emotionally or psychologically? Yes, you will feel better, again, temporarily, but for how long? I'd much rather own the restaurant than boast about eating at the restaurant, but maybe I'm just the crazy one. Escaping to a lavish vacation on an island to make my mind feel better in a financially stressful situation, or looking good and dining with the upscalers, or spending hundreds or thousands of dollars at the club but not having an investment portfolio are the keys to balling backwards. I know this from experience; this was once me.

Not everybody who enjoys nice things are "escaping financial stress," but I do see an honest trend of things or actions that look good based on removed external perception but in reality, they are totally backwards. If things in your life look good online, or they look captivating to the world, even as a cover up, that is OK. Why? Remember, nobody ever taught us financial intelligence. One of the important concepts I will stress in this book is OWNERSHIP. OWN things first then nice stuff comes later. In fact, I will discuss the importance of equity in detail later on in this book.

I must also say that this book is not intended to give investment advice, stock tips, guidance about performance, or anything of that nature. I am not currently licensed or in a position to give investment recommendations, nor do I want to be. This book is about changing one's MINDSET and recognizing that there ARE many opportunities to change financial habits if you have access to the information and have your mind over money mindset.

The financially illiterate American

Almost 70% of ALL Americans have $1,000 or less in a savings account, or saved up, and 34% have no savings at all! Did you know that? Is that you? There are many research studies that show that the average American is horribly uneducated in the areas of financial literacy. What's worse is that in the African-American community, data shows that the average family has less wealth than any other racial or ethnic group. That has to start changing NOW.

In a 2015 study conducted by the National Capability Study, researchers interviewed participants between the months of June and October. The investigators discovered that out of over 27,000 respondents, almost two-thirds of them could only get 1 or 2 questions right from a 5 question BASIC financial literacy test. It is worth noting that this was not a 5-hour series 7 exam where the test taker has to almost strip down naked and can't even bring a bottle of water in when taking the test (they take cheating prevention to another level; I didn't know if I was on an intake jail block or if I was in a testing center).

Questions on the aforementioned exam would ask: "If you take out a $1,000 loan that has a 20% interest rate, how much will you owe a year in interest?" Amazingly, many people did not know that $200 was the correct answer without having to "Google it." Again, isn't it great that we can use Google to find out everything? I remember when you had to go to the library to get information and use Dewey decimals and big encyclopedias to look up information. The fact that the average American can't even pass a minimum basic financial literacy test is worth a larger discussion, especially when the topic impacts almost every aspect of our lives.

The worst part about the findings from this and other studies is that this is just the tip of the iceberg. Whether it be the topic of saving, investing (most Americans know nothing about the stock market nor do they participate, which can immediately impact your wealth accumulation) or "common" things such as interest rates and mortgage rates, most people have no clue about what these concepts actually mean and how to use them to their advantage.

Again, Mind Over Money is not about giving graphs that state a lot of techno babble, although I do think that obtaining skilled information is extremely helpful; instead, this book is about a mindset and paradigm shift that gives you the ability to take action no matter what financial state you are currently in. Whether you make $8 an hour and have very little income (they actually have apps now where you can invest as little as $5 which makes you an immediate equity share holder) or you are making over six figures and are scratching your head on why you are still living check to check, this book can help you. Again, if that is you then you are completely normal, especially since over one-third of those who make 100k a year are still living check to check.

The good news is that this book will give you steps to take immediate action. If you find yourself somewhere in the middle, don't worry, this book is still for you and will give you all of the tools that you need to get serious about creating generational wealth and leaving a legacy for your family. As you read each chapter of the book, think about how it applies to you. Most importantly, engage in the advice given and take the required steps to change your MINDSET and to change your life.

CHAPTER 2 – WHY ECONOMICS AND FINANCIAL LITERACY ARE SO IMPORTANT

Right now, you may not be sold on why I believe that the key to financial literacy is more than just learning some new concepts and applying them. You may also be perplexed as to why I am stressing a complete shift in how you live your life. Fair enough. Let me share a few more points with you.

First and foremost, America is a culture in which money controls everything. Money controls almost all access to every resource—just think about it. Look around where you are right now. Whether it is in your home, in an office, on a bus, in a coffee shop, or on a plane— money controlled how it was built and why it was built. Looking at it from an international perspective, it is even more transparent.

I know you're probably reading this and it may sound all well and good, but you may want to know why I feel capable to deliver this life changing message. Rightfully so, you are probably wondering: What is my story?

I am a former licensed securities agent who worked in corporate America as an investment professional for over 5 years; I studied finance at a very high level. I have worked with all types of accounts such as personal savings, retirement, IRAs (traditional and Roth), 529 Plans, ESAs (Education Savings Accounts), custodial accounts, trust accounts, estate accounts, etc.

In addition, I have traded securities such as stocks, bonds, mutual funds, ETFs, and many other types of securities. I have worked with multi-million-dollar clients on a daily basis and I have seen up close and personal how the financial markets work. I have also seen the huge gap in this financial knowledge and how the average American knows little about financial literacy and little about how money is leveraged to build wealth.

I have since left corporate America, and I am now currently the Founder and Chief Executive Officer of McCrary Financial Solutions, LLC which owns The McCrary Financial School. I now educate thousands of people digitally about the concepts of financial intelligence and how to build generational wealth. This is my story and why I am so passionate about shifting the paradigm for the better.

I must also say that I am NOT a believer of the MONEY IS EVERYTHING AND THE MONEY OVER EVERYTHING PHILOSPHY. I want to make this crystal clear because I want you to look at this book from an uncommon viewpoint and understand the ways in which I view money and my relationship with money. My epiphany that I could not buy into the money over everything philosophy came from my experiences while still working in corporate America. Let me explain.

I graduated from college in 2011 right after the turmoil of the 2008 crash and the Great Recession, which was the worst national financial state since the Great Depression of the 1930s. This was a time in which jobs weren't as easy to get and having a college degree didn't hold nearly as much weight as it used to. This also led many companies to do business in different ways, given the unpredictable financial times. After months of looking for jobs in the sociology and social work fields, I wasn't having any luck.

I went on so many job interviews and tried to put my best suit on, be clean-shaved, and sound super impressive in those STAR (situation, task, action, result) question interviews but I was still having no luck. I came to the realization that in the social services field, the people who were more likely to get the job were people with previous experience or a Master's degree; I had neither.

After months and months of job rejections, I finally got a job working as an annuity case manager then as an investment professional at a very well-known firm that has AUM (assets under management) of close to 5 Trillion Dollars. This job did not care if you had a previous background in finance because they provided on-the-job training to give you the skills and tools needed to do the job efficiently.

YES! I made it right? I got that fancy corporate job with benefits and a good salary, etc.? That's what we go to school for, right? I MADE IT! WOO HOO! Initially, that's exactly how I felt, but as the years progressed, my happiness and sense of achievement started fading and fading. I say this all to say that after my 5 years of working in corporate America, I *know* for a fact that if I truly believed in the money over everything philosophy, I could have gotten a big salary making well over 6 figures with a corner office and be that token that every company points to in order to meet their "diversity clause," but I would have had to change the person that I am.

Keep in mind that I don't look down on ANYONE in a high place in the corporate world; I can just say that from my experiences, I saw the horse and jockey corporate dynamic and I was damned if I was going to play the role as the horse and let someone else be the jockey.

I say all of this to say that at the same time, as my experiences have shaped the way I look at money and what I choose to do to earn money, I still believe that money is not everything, but it ALMOST IS. Also, now that I am a business owner, my daily routine constantly revolves around MAKING MONEY because as all business owners know, without revenue you have no business. It is as simple as that.

I say that money is ALMOST everything because there are millions of people who have boats of money, but they are not happy at all. In order to paint a crisper picture, let's look at the role that money plays in most people's life.

Think about how you live your life. If you are like most Americans, when you first wake up, most of us have to get up and go to work. Ah ha! Immediately, when we wake up, we are automatically triggered to do SOMETHING TO MAKE MONEY! This leads to an interesting relationship between many people and their place of employment.

If you are a full-time employee or even an entrepreneur, you must ask: Is the work you do everyday something you are truly passionate about? If you are, then great! I personally LOVE what I do as an entrepreneur, but as an employee, I didn't. Research shows that an American's satisfaction with a job depends on many different factors such as whether they are salaried or hourly, the industry that they are in, and if it is a service vs corporate sector. But a statistic that stood out to me, from research done in October 2016 by Pew Research Center, showed that 30% of Americans say that their job is just a job "to get by". Let that sink in—30% or one-third of us are working just to work. This equates to millions of people who are in jobs that they probably despise.

Why do some people continue to do these jobs then? Because they need MONEY! When you meet someone for the first time or even when you see some of your relatives that you haven't seen in a while, what is usually one of the first questions they ask you?

If it is a new contact, they may ask: "So, what do you do?" "Where do you work?" "What do you do for a living?" These questions are common because we mistakenly think that they define who we are, right?

A family member, after they first ask how you are, may immediately ask something like: "How's work?" "How's your job?" Or, if you don't have a "job" or something good to tell them "work related," their body language starts to change and they start looking at you in a different way. Why is that?

As an entrepreneur now, I actually hate this script and since I have shifted my mindset to having a deeper purpose in life than just rising up the corporate ladder, I HATE when people ask me: How's your job? Most people can't understand the fact that a job can be created and we don't always have to work for someone else.

I do not hate it because I don't have anything great to share about the work I do. I actually over deliver information to the point that the person who asks me will often walk away like *WOW his work is much deeper than anything I ever imagined*. But I hate it because why should having a fancy corporate job or having a job with prestige or status completely define who you are?

Think about someone like Muhammed Ali. He is probably the greatest athlete, not just boxer, of all time. As great as he was, I personally think that what he did as a man is far greater than anything he did as an athlete. Yes, he made history in sports, but the legacy he left in fighting for the black community, to change the racial dynamic, is unprecedented. I could go on and on about celebrities or other successful people and I believe that deep down inside, they would also tell you that how the world views them is only a small microcosm of who they truly are as individuals. Lebron James is currently my favorite athlete and he is probably the 2nd best basketball player of all time, but I think what he does off of the court is equally, if not more, impressive.

The reason why where you work and "what you do" is so important to us is because for most of us, it is the lifeblood of how we financially survive. If you are one of those people in which your job is the lifeblood of your life and you cannot financially function without it, but you are also in the 30% who are "just [getting] by" or you hate your job, have you ever seriously thought about other ways to earn a living outside of your 9-5? I mean that job didn't just appear out of thin air; someone had to *create* that job. Did you ever seriously look into what it would take for you to create that job for yourself? By the end of this book, you will have answers for that question.

Entrepreneurship is a big slice of the financial pie. If you have your mind over money, instead of waking up every day and thinking immediately about MONEY and your job to MAKE MONEY or doing something you really don't want to do for MONEY, consider thinking about your passion: What if your passion came FIRST then creating money from your PASSION? In other words, I encourage you to spend that SAME amount of time and energy using your MIND before thinking about money. Of course, you will be thinking about ways to make money, but let's take money out of it and think about what it would take to survive if you didn't have money or had to do something you didn't desire to do to earn money.

Automatically, the paradigm shifts and you start to think about money and earning differently. Just imaging spending that same 8 or 12 hours as an internal think tank, thinking about all of the ways to obtain resources and to function besides working your day to day job. Once you start thinking this way, you will see a new world of opportunities and tangible results come your way.

I know all too well about the "blowing money fast" syndrome and the "spend it all because I can't take it with me" culture—both consist of spending money carelessly and fearlessly. For the people who say I'm going to spend it all because "I can't take it with me" yes, that's true you can't take it with you, but can't you pass it down to your children? If you don't have any children, don't you have other relatives or something else constructive to do with your funds to have positive impact instead of making someone else rich? I have been around celebrities and people who you would think were doing well financially, or people who just spend money like water but don't have anything on the balance sheet to show for it.

When given the opportunity, I often engage in casual conversations and small talk to try to bring to the forefront the importance of having smart spending habits and it rarely ever sticks as something interesting to talk about. Why is that? Like I said before, since financial literacy and how we spend money pretty much controls every aspect of our life, including how we eat, healthcare, education for our children, etc., why is it that we don't find it interesting to discuss financial literacy?

And even when we have someone giving out this important knowledge, many of us won't even attend a free seminar, but we will spend hundreds of dollars to make someone else rich, just to be ENTERTAINED. Are we that brainwashed? Do we not want to know the important stuff that is really going to impact our lives? Why would we much rather talk about sports and analyzing football stats than to talk about building and helping each other leave a legacy for our families? I know that the sports team owners are making sure that their finances are in top order, so why would we spend hours counting their money, but we won't spend 5 minutes counting our own?

This is why this stuff is so important. I've seen people with multiple children brag about how much money they blew at the mall or the nice car they just got and I think to myself, well can your kids eat a car? Can you pass it down? If you have nice shiny things but don't have stocks for your kids or 529 college plans please make changes immediately. You owe it to them. If you are reading this and you don't have any children, think to yourself, do you want children one day? If the answer is yes, you are still already too late, you need to be planning for your unborn children NOW.

I hope it's starting to get clearer as to why this "financial literacy stuff" is so important and why these conversations need to be at the forefront of our everyday discussions. I also would like to emphasize that this DOES NOT mean that you should not enjoy nice things, not by any stretch. I LOVE nice shiny fancy things, but at the same time, the goal is to take care of business first. Once you have your mind over money, you will take care of business first and have plenty left over to feed your lavish cravings. I will not buy anything nice if I don't have an investment portfolio; it is as simple as that.

PAY YOURSELF FIRST

Now let's discuss why it is so important to PAY YOURSELF FIRST. Many people balance their budget like this:

Most people pay all of their bills first, then pay for wants or desires (leisure or play money) then MAYBE put stuff away for themselves in savings or a few dollars to invest.

You actually should be doing the opposite. But once you change your mindset, all you have to do is redirect those dollars. Those same funds you use for fast food or going out to eat, coffee, or leisure items, etc. - if you reduce those amenities and redirect those dollars, you can instantly start a nice nest egg for a rainy day. It can be just as simple as that, but are you up for the mental challenge to redirect and keep those dollars safe? I hope so. We owe it to our kids. Just DON'T go out to eat as much or start with eating fast food one less time and USE that MONEY FOR YOURSELF!

If you want to take it further, as soon as you get your income, PAY YOURSELF FIRST! Set aside 10% immediately and put it into savings, investing, etc., again IN YOURSELF!

Once you understand the power of redirecting, you will see that no matter what financial state you are in, you can take immediate steps to enhance your financial situation. This is why engaging in thoughtful discussions, followed by execution is so important. Economics and finance control our everyday lives.

How other successful and financially independent people live their lives.

Another important factor to getting ahead financially is to study how financially successful people live their lives. Study how they move.

Look at what they do. What is their day to day life like? How do they view money? What do they do with their time? What goals do they have for their life? What books do they read? What seeds are they planting today that will have an impact on the way our future shapes up. There is a lot of talk about Donald Trump, but no one talks about the seeds that his father planted years earlier to give him the ability to be in control of the free world. People look at the tree, but they rarely ever study the roots.

If you truly want to get ahead, which I know is the case because you are reading this book, I want you to look at how these people move, but don't stop there. I want you to try to get around these people. It may even take some years but make a constant effort to be around and in the same room as people who are financially ahead. Remember if you are the smartest one in the room, you are in the wrong room. Find out what books they are reading and go out and purchase them and then read the same books they are reading. The internet and social media make it vastly easier to seek out these individuals and get close to them, even if it can only be done digitally or virtually.

Most of the great relationships that I have now took years to acquire and thousands of dollars well spent as well. Investing in relationships and information from people who have already been where you are trying to go will save you years of trial and error and save you massive amounts of money on the back end.

CHAPTER 3 – THE MIND OVER MONEY PRINCIPLE

In this chapter, I will introduce you to the Mind Over Money principle which will give you the keys to achieving financial freedom. Having your mind over your money is all about thinking about your financial decisions from an unselfish perspective. It's about putting your priorities first and emotions later. Now I know this may be a hard principle to grasp because we all feel so good when we are able to purchase the things that we want, even if we get the short end of the stick in the long run.

Sales are emotional

Being an entrepreneur now has led me to learn the science behind sales and marketing. Most spending is emotional. That is why we feel so good when we buy something. Retail therapy, right? When we first walk into that department store and someone greets us at the door or says a nice compliment to us. That is all intended to make us feel good and make us feel more inclined to purchase from their store. I've heard many people that just came back from spending a lot of money, and then they say "the people in the store were so nice to me!" Of course, they were! They want your money!

There was a video produced around the 1960s titled: "How to sell to the Negro." It was all about how to sell to the African-American community. It showed how he "wanted to feel important" and how to "make him feel special to get his money." That's the same model most corporations use to get the black dollar today. There are many people who say that many blacks have low self-esteem and don't feel important and companies use that to their advantage to get our money, which I do, to an extent, agree with, but at the same time, I believe we have the responsibility to combat that and take care of business first. And we control that. Let me explain.

I find it interesting that blacks are more likely to have luxury cars than any other race; we are also the demographic most likely to buy a product just because a celebrity endorsed it [around 25% of ALL NIKES are sold to African-Americans!] Let me repeat that: We buy 25% of all Nikes!!!! Nike is an international brand that sells sneakers in more countries than their competitors, yet 25% of all of their products are sold to the African-American community. Yet, we only own one-half of 1% of the nation's wealth in the richest country on earth. This highlights why we need to have our mind over our money and take care of business first in order to create wealth for future generations. Now I want to break down almost every aspect of our financial life and show you that if you apply the mind over money principle, you will shift the paradigm immediately.

The Mind Over Money Principle for Living

One of the biggest expenses most people have is living expenses. There is a wide debate about renting vs. owning and which one makes more financial sense. While I do believe that decision is mostly subjective and about preference and each specific situation is different, financial data proves that just from an economics or financially intelligent perspective based on numbers, owning is a much smarter decision in the long run. Again, we are thinking for the long term; get rich quick schemes fade fast and running your financial life only from a daily or weekly perspective is a fast way to start robbing Peter to pay Paul. Let's not rob anyone and pay ourselves first.

On one side of the argument, yes, renting *can* be more cost effective because of not having the obligation for property maintenance, home insurance , taxes, or any unexpected expenses that come from being a property owner. You also have more freedom to move whenever you please and are not locked into a 30-year fixed mortgage.

On the other side of the argument, owning a house or property gives you the ability to build up equity; you get tax breaks that you don't have access to when you only rent. Also, real estate can be passed down to future generations, and of course you can also rent out your property and gain residual income.

You can also buy a duplex and rent other units out to almost live for free and have your tenants pay you rent which then pays off your mortgage. You can also utilize section 8 housing to guarantee a check for yourself at the first of every month. These are just some of the many resources that you can use to your advantage simply for being a property owner.

Now it is not my job to tell you *how* to live or which is RIGHT or

WRONG. I just want to lay out a lot of information for you to think about when it comes to living a financially literate life. Numbers show that when you rent for a long period of time, you actually have bought your landlord that house or maybe two. And let's not even discuss compound interest, meaning that if that same landlord were to take that monthly income he receives and invests it in the stock market, he could tally up close to half a million dollars. But buying a house is too hard right? "I just want to take the easy route and just coming up with first month, last month, and security," but in the long run you are losing hundreds of thousands of dollars.

For example, if you pay $1000 in rent for 20 years, that's $240,000 you paid in rent! What do you have to show for it? Sure, you may have a beautiful apartment, loft, or condo, etc. but I mean what do you have that is tangible? Do you have equity? Can you pass that house down to someone else, or if your child needs somewhere to live can you give them that property?

One of the biggest things people miss when it comes to home ownership is the power of owning a duplex. This is something that needs to be discussed more to recognize the opportunities for other resources and money we can earn for thinking outside the box. Like I said earlier, owning a duplex or multi family unit can possibly give you the ability to earn residual monthly income or at minimum almost live for free. Wouldn't you want to live for free? Imagine getting monthly rental checks from your tenants that would actually cover your entire mortgage and some, and you still own the property! It's not that far-fetched, go out and look into acquiring and owning a duplex.

Now this not telling you WHAT to do or that renting is a bad decision, by no means at all. But let's look at who are the ones who traditionally get ahead in America. The people who get ahead in America are the people who do and own 3 things:

1). People who own businesses

2). People who invest (stocks, bonds, mutual funds, etc.)

3). People who own real estate

So, I would say to you, do you own any of these three? If you don't own any properties, do you own any stocks or investments? Do you own a business or have an equity share in a business? On the flip side if you do own real estate, is that your only investment or asset that you own?

The great Robert Kiyosaki says that if your home is your greatest asset than you are in bad shape, and of course we would never question the Godfather of asset accumulation, money management, and the cashflow quadrant, but I would say that if you do own your home and that is your only asset, you are still a step above those who don't own any assets and still rent an apartment.

The most important part of all of this again is not to tell you what to do, but to remind you that you should be thinking about ALL of this when it comes to how you live and how much you spend on living expenses.

I am seeing a lot of new home owners and I love it; people are making plans, saving money and executing on buying a house. I love delayed gratification or making plans and executing on those plans. We need more of that. I would also like to encourage those folks not to stop there and to go out and buy some stocks and look into business ownership. Collectively, this is how you can truly build generational wealth.

The Mind Over Money Principle for Cars

Let me just get the elephant out of the book now. Wealth has nothing to do with a nice car, house, jewelry, or any other material items that do not appreciate in value. **A CAR IS NOT WEALTH**. I see too many people brag about the car they have, or making it seem like they have a lot of money because of the car they drive. Once again, **A CAR IS NOT WEALTH**. If you own a luxury car but you don't own a house, go take your car back. If you own a Gucci bag but don't own any stocks, please go take your bag back and go open a brokerage stock portfolio.

I'm tired of seeing people settling for being "hood rich." Hood rich is when you have lots of cars, clothes, or jewelry, but have no equity, no investments, no private equity, no venture capital firms in your rolodex, no will, no trusts, no estate planning, and no life insurance. If you have a luxury car but no life insurance, again you are balling backwards.

All of the successful people that I KNOW that I KNOW have money, whether they own multi-million-dollar businesses, real estate, or heavy investment portfolios, never talk about their cars. I'm sure they have very nice cars, but it has never once been an interesting topic to discuss. Instead, they talk about multi-million-dollar acquisitions, or real estate investment trust deals. Or they discuss how to build a multi-million-dollar digital brand. They never once talk about their car and "how much money they have because of the car they drive."

I say that a car is not wealth because it is not an asset. As soon as you buy a new car and drive it off the lot, it immediately depreciates in value. In order to get ahead financially, we need to be thinking about putting our money into things that appreciate in value not things that don't. Stocks, real estate, businesses, artwork, etc. have the ability to appreciate in value, cars, clothes, and jewelry do not.

When you apply the mind over money principle, you understand that it doesn't mean that you can't buy an expensive car, it just means that you buy the nice car AFTER we have an EMERGENCY savings fund. We purchase the nice car AFTER we own the stocks and bonds. We buy the car AFTER we have money tucked away for our kids and after we have equity in land or property. The mind over money principle is about taking care of business FIRST and buying the WANTS later. No flash now and time will reveal money.

The Mind over Money Principle for consumer items

When it pertains to other material or consumer items, the Mind Over Money Principle is similar to how we view the car that we drive. We know that we buy the material items and consumer items AFTER we invest for our children. We spend hundreds or thousands at the mall, AFTER we buy the property and so on and so forth. Once you apply this new mindset, you will see that it doesn't have to be one or the other, you cake actually have your cake and eat it to.

The Mind over Money Principle for ENTERTAINMENT

One of the main things that troubles me the most about the African-American community is how much we consume entertainment. We consume and spend money on entertainment far more than any other group; yet, we have less wealth than any other group. Is there a correlation between that, or is it by coincidence?

Again, this is not to down anyone who spends the whole weekend binging on Netflix or spending money on entertainment. This is for the people who want more out of life and who recognize the need to make some changes. I speak for the people who want to be highly successful, not individuals who think that their success starts and stops with a

MEME about how they want to be a millionaire. If you want to achieve high levels of success, do you spend more time watching a basketball game, or reading a book written by someone who achieved success and gives you the steps and actions they took in order to make that dream a reality? How bad do you want it?

I also think it is unhealthy for our community to let media control so many facets of our life. What I mean by that is if you base a relationship on what you see on a reality TV show, you need to turn off the TV and get back down to reality.

The mind over money principle for entertainment means that if we are going to spend 4 hours watching ESPN or SportsCenter back to back, we are also going to own a share of stock in Disney, since they are the parent company of ESPN. It also means that if we are going to set a reminder on our phone every Monday at 8PM to watch *Love and Hip Hop*, we are also going to make sure we own shares of Viacom which is the parent company of VH1. I guarantee that those shares of stock will be less than your cable bill.

While we are on the subject of stock ownership, did you know that a share of stock costs less than a pair of Jordan's? Did you know that a share of stock in Apple costs less than the iPhone X? So why aren't we buying the shares of stock along with the consumer products? Yes, it is a lack of information, but now that we have the information, why aren't we doing it?

I hope that I have summed up SOME of the ways you can shift the paradigm to start spending and living your life differently. Again, there is a way to have your cake and eat it too. We could literally go into every aspect of how people spend money and go into detail about how to redirect almost all of our dollars, but I just wanted to lay out the main expenses we normally spend money on, and how a simple shift could save you potentially hundreds of thousands of dollars.

CHAPTER 4 – HOW TO AVOID BEING STUCK IN THE PAST

Now that you have a basic understanding of the Mind Over Money principle, I want to dive in and analyze the world in which we currently live and how it relates to the previous points that I have raised in the book.

Too many of us are walking around like it's still the 20th century or even the early 2000s. Remember the dotcom bubble? At that time, we thought we were so far into the future and how far ahead we were. Yes, we did come a long way, but looking back at the early 2000s now, even 15 years ago seems like ancient times compared to today. I say that many people are still stuck in the past because the way they live their life, make money, and how they look at the way they THINK the world works is one that is stuck on out of date times.

The direct to consumer relationship

There once was a time in which we *had* to go through a middle man or higher up just to get our message out to the world. Whether it was a new business product or an idea that we thought might "change the world" we *had* to go through a middle man just to get it out to the masses. Those days, my friend, are long gone and have little hope to return.

For example, if you wanted to put a movie out, or you wanted to be the next Ralph Lauren, you almost had no choice but to get Macys or Lord and Taylor on board to *let* you into their store in order to sell your clothing products. You had to come up with the right sales pitch or to convince that VP to put your product launch into the store because we had miniscule ways to a large group of people. It was a very challenging uphill battle to get customers on our own. Once again, those time are long gone and don't see any glimmer to return; let me explain.

With the evolution of technology, now if you want to start a clothing store all you have to do is go on Shopify or Big Cartel and start your own online store in a matter of minutes. And the kicker is the management fee to run the store is probably less than your phone bill! Sidebar - Did you know that Shopify had over 400k in sales per minute go through their company during BFCM (Black Friday and Cyber Monday) weekend! That is amazing considering this company didn't even exist 15 years ago. [This company only opened in 2004.]

We live in an age where we now have a direct-to-consumer relationship in which we can directly talk and get to our fans or customers. This is something that most traditional employees don't even realize and miss out on thousands if not millions of dollars. The internet and social media gives us the ability to cut out the middle men and get our message out in an entirely new fashion.

A great resource if you would like to go more in-depth to learn about the power of social media and how to cut out the middle man is to read *The Gatekeepers are Gone* by Lamar Tyler. Lamar Tyler is the founder of *Traffic, Sales, and Profit* and *Black and Married with Kids.com*. His teachings have literally changed my life and my business.

When you realize these new opportunities, you realize how shallow it is just to use social media to take a few cute pictures to put on Instagram or only to use social media to rant about something unpleasant in your life. The evolutions of the internet and social media have literally destroyed previous industries and built brand new ones. We all need to be on board to ride this new wave and cash out on digital opportunities. Whether you are a professor, media personality, chef, or sales expert, social media gives you the ability to build and have your own platform and directly market to your fans without a middle man.

Today, a professor doesn't have to brown nose for tenure, he can do a Facebook live video and teach people all across the world. An aspiring chef doesn't have to put all of his hopes into a casting call to appear on a TV Food show, he can start a YouTube channel and cook from his own kitchen and reach millions of people with the right Google Ad Words Campaign. Again, we live in a completely different world than the past, but are you taking full advantage of the opportunities or are you letting them pass you by and letting someone else giving you a paycheck dictate your household?

This particularly works well for me because one of my main career goals was to become a financial advisor. I played the corporate game of getting to work early, requesting to stay late to "help out", engaging in weird corporate activities, building relationships in the company, etc. At the time, I thought this would translate to being promoted to becoming a CFP or financial advisor but the reality of racism in corporate America overshadowed whatever hopes and dreams I thought I would achieve.

No matter how many interviews I went on, (yes, I had to go on an interview just to get a higher position in the same company), I used to think, "These people act as if I am not already an employee of this company the way they make it so hard to move up." I could literally write an entire book about the ills of Corporate America, maybe look out for that in the near future, but I did everything that was "required" and more to "be the best candidate" or do what I saw my white counterparts do in order to get those positions, but I was still not let into that circle. No matter how many times I tried, I would still get that email that read "We LOVED your interview, **BUT** we decided to go with another candidate—someone else we felt was more suitable for the position." BS, right? Have you ever experienced this?

I have to honestly say that was a very stressful time. I thought that in order to fulfill my own dreams, I had to be *given* the opportunity to be *allowed* to move up. I had high dreams of becoming a "top financial advisor" and give customers "great financial advice." I wanted to be an example of why this company was the best in the business and that "hard work really does pay off."

I look back now, laugh, and thank God I did not get that position. Now, I don't *HAVE* to *ask* anyone to make me an advisor, I don't have to *ask* anyone if I can get *permission* to share important financial information. I now can go on Facebook Live and talk directly to my people and I can reach people all around the world at the snap of a finger! Isn't that amazing! Are you using technology to your advantage in order to get your message for the world out?

I love the fact that I get messages and emails from people in London, Africa, California, Texas, the Caribbean, etc. that watch my videos and tell me how it has helped improve their financial life. This is what really drives my passion. If there was no direct-to-consumer relationship, I would probably still be stuck on the corporate ladder waiting for someone to "give me a chance" to do something great.

Now, let me reemphasize: I am not a financial advisor, as I said in the beginning of the book, I am not licensed to nor do I want to be giving advice or portfolio recommendations. But I am a financial coach and I do teach financial literacy. I teach important strategies you can use to get ahead based on my years of experience working in the finance industry and now I don't have to ask anyone to do that. It's interesting also that online entrepreneurs actually make far more money than investment advisors anyway. I was so caught up on getting a promotion because I thought it would be a big pay day, only to learn that the real money is in entrepreneurship through technology, not a fancy position with a nice salary. Sometimes when we don't get an opportunity, it can actually be a blessing in disguise or open up a door to a better solution. Rather than being resentful or upset, see a potential let down as an opportunity to grow and get better.

Education and learning in today's environment

Education and the way we consume information is also something that I believe needs to be looked at from a non-traditional perspective.

First and foremost, there is a big difference between having a degree and being educated. One of my all-time favorite leaders was Malcolm X, who never went past the 8th grade, yet he was more educated than many PhDs. He didn't even get a high school diploma; yet, he held lectures on Ivy League campuses. Nowadays, with the evolution of the internet and social media, it is easier to obtain information than ever before.

Getting a degree is good and can be very useful in helping you get to a certain career goal, but I truly think the whole model of education needs to be re-evaluated and put into perspective for the current time that we live in.

Unlike ever before, there is so much FREE education you can obtain just from the cell phone that you hold in your hand. Google is literally a university. You can learn so much valuable and relevant information that you can actually apply in everyday life. This is not to mention "YouTube University" - yes, I call it YouTube University. If you care to look at it as a digital classroom instead of *only* looking at it to get a good laugh or listen to your favorite musical artist, you will begin to see its virtual classrooms.

People have told me that I am an early adopter because I am on the new wave of technology, but I also see it from both perspectives. I grew up with the traditional mindset that doing K-12 and then going to college was the "most important" thing you had to do in order to "get a job" and have a nice SUCCESSFUL LIFE. Think about how much emphasis we put on college? I too back then thought that the only way to get ahead in life was to go to college. This is why I went to obtain my Bachelor of Arts degree in sociology. Bear with me as I explain how my position on college has vastly changed and why the shift has occurred.

Like I stated before, I grew up like many other people, believing how important college was and how that was going to set me up for success. Now let me say that I am not anti-college at all. I still think that college is very important, but the way we look at it needs to be re-evaluated.

1) **The cost of education has VASTLY increased and job wages have not.**

So, number one, for us to keep going off "what previous generations did" and how just because someone in the family went to college it changed the family dynamic, that is nice but can be seen as outdated given the current times we live in in the 21st century and will be approaching a new decade soon.

College is nowhere near what it used to cost and many universities are literally robbing students blind while they are under a construction BOOM with new buildings. Take a look at almost all colleges especially in urban areas and you will see a lot of cranes and construction workers building brand new buildings from the overpricing of tuition. It is like the industrial revolution of the 19th and 20th century all over again only this time it is led by the colleges and universities. Nobody should have to spend more than $20,000 a year to get an education. It is fair to say that is strong-arm robbery. Why should someone come out with a mortgage debt with no house to show for it? It is not fair and this crisis needs to be discussed more often with real policy to correct this error in education.

What's worse than that is even when you take on that debt and get your degree, it's not that simple to find a job and if you do, many jobs don't pay what you need to live let alone be able to afford monthly student loan repayment expenses.

Being part of the millennial generation, I am right in the middle of this crisis. I see what is going on and am trying to be at the forefront of implementing a new ideology. They say that the average millennial is going to die in debt. DIE IN DEBT??? Do you think that is fair? Every generation in history has traditionally done better than their parents; this is the first generation where we might actually be going backwards.

So, with this being said and with understanding all of the things that are going on and "not being stuck in the past" and "thinking like we are still in the past," I want us to also think about how we can do things smarter in order to truly get ahead in this lifetime. For example, the internet provides us with the resources to get the information without being a slave to Sallie Mae or any other lender for that matter.

My thoughts for implementing a SMART and strategic new way of thinking is to number one think about what we want to do in life. For jobs such as doctors, lawyers, engineers, etc., yes you HAVE to get a degree and that degree gets you in that field, and most of those jobs pay you a good salary in order to pay back your loans. But I do think it is not a smart financial decision to go into a large amount of debt to get a job that barely pays you enough to survive or doesn't give you enough to feed your family and you die in debt. In a country as rich as ours, I think that there are better ways to go about it.

2) **Often, the information we learn in college doesn't give us the knowledge we need to fully thrive in society. So, I believe this also needs to be re-evaluated and integrated into financial literacy and other important financial topics that we should learn about.**

We need to be learning how to buy a house, how to start an investment portfolio, how to be able to capitalize on waves such as Bitcoin or another Cryptocurrency. We need to be learning how to develop a business and how to market and sell products. I truly believe that this would be more beneficial than writing a 15-page paper about stuff we won't even remember the next semester.

So, I say to current or future college students, make sure you take time to learn what you *really* will need for the real world because whether you like it or not you will NEED it - it is as simple as that. So, whether you prepare now or prepare later, at some point in your life you will need to learn real world financial information.

I say this all to say that when you understand what is currently going on and you are not stuck in the past, you will learn that there is so much valuable information you can learn through online trainings and online programs. Of course, YouTube and Google are free, and can give you vital information, but there are paid online courses than put traditional college courses to shame. There are online business programs that may cost you a few thousand bucks but will help you far more than that $30,000 a year you will spend to write a bunch of research papers. Once you start getting into digital learning you will see how far ahead of its time it is.

The fact that I can wake up and learn while still in my pajamas - learn critical information again literally in my pajamas is revolutionary. And it can be revolutionary for you too! And many of these programs are self-study so you can fully consume the content at your own pace. We as a human race receive and consume information unlike ever before but it's all about recognizing the power of technology and using it to your advantage to get the real nuggets from those who are so gracious to share them.

The digital economy – The way in which we earn a living

With the evolution of the internet and social media, the way we can earn a living has changed tremendously . I honestly don't think many people understand this important life shift. The fact that someone has the ability to earn a living on an Instagram app instead of going to punch a clock at a 9-5 is amazing to say the least, and I don't think most people grasp how dynamic that is.

Look at the Lavar Ball situation for instance. Many people who are "stuck in the past" would call him crazy for not wanting to sign with Nike or Adidas, but he is smart enough to recognize the times that you no longer have to sign your life away to these big corporations. Lavar

Ball is controversial yes, but brilliant at recognizing the direct-to-consumer relationship we discussed a few pages ago. He knows that now you no longer *have* to get Nike to distribute your sneakers; you can now open up your own online store and sell directly to your millions of followers on Facebook and Instagram. This could not have been done in previous generations.

Again, there were times when we *had* to work in that factory or that corporation because there were only limited opportunities to earn income in other ways. Now, with a laptop and smartphone, you don't even have to be in a specific location to earn a living, you can be a digital nomad and run an online business and not be tied to a desk to earn a paycheck. I truly believe that if the only way you can earn a living is defined by your location, you are operating from a place in the past and you are limiting your ability to be successful and profitable.

The digital economy has opened the cash registers to endless possibilities that give you no excuse to be able to make things happen. You can sell products and services all over the world and never have to be in a remote location. The evolution of Facebook advertising is also something you need to be fully aware of and how to use it to your advantage.

Facebook advertising is something else that does not get the type of attention that we need to give it. So, by now, you may be thinking: "Ok, Ryan but just because I have a social media page, how do I get my message to the masses even when I have a small following?" Well now we can actually BUY attention to get our product/services or message out to the world unlike ever before. Think about in past years, if we wanted to get out a new product or an important message, how would we get it out to the masses? We would do radio or TV ads or take out an ad in the local or national newspaper. This is straight forward, right? The problem with this is that most big platforms were ridiculously expensive to get access to, and we also needed to be *approved* to get on TV or radio. We would have to get approval from those "gatekeepers" or middle men because they had access to the people. It was very hard to go around that and get access to an audience, which could make or break whether our message would be heard.

Now, with the enormous empire that Facebook has built, and the amount of data they have access to, now almost ANYONE has the ability to advertise off Facebook and reach enormous amounts of people if done correctly. The fact that I don't have to beg to get on TV or go through hoops to get on the radio, and I can reach millions of people through Facebook advertising is unprecedented. By taking advantage of these advancements, it puts you into the future and keeps you from being stuck in the past. Whether you advertise through Facebook or Instagram, and now you can even advertise on Facebook Messenger, you have the ability to create your own opportunities. But it's all about recognizing these opportunities and not holding on to ancient thinking that keeps you stuck in the past.

CHAPTER 5 – THE ESSENCE OF TIME

One of the biggest aspects of life that many people take for granted is the essence of TIME. Knowing how precious TIME really is and recognizing the power of time is what separates many dreams from reality. I am a strong believer that the greatest asset that any human possesses is TIME. Without time we don't have anything. Once you understand the correct relationship between time and money, you will live your life from a completely different perspective and you will never see either time or money the same way.

Now I know this book is about money and making smart decisions when it pertains to money, but what you do with your time is equally if not more important than money. Even if you currently have no money I guarantee there is valuable time sitting under you that can be turned into dollars if done the correct way. Many people that do not have a lot of money actually have a lot of TIME but the problem is they do not see value in this spare time.

TIME is something that every person reading this book has, some may have more TIME than others but ultimately if you are still on this earth you have some time of some sort. This is why if you want to be highly successful you cannot waste ANY time! Why do many people let a corporation put a price tag on their time, but they don't use that time to build a corporation for themselves? Why would you work harder for someone else than you do for yourself? People who get ahead financially are those that maximize their time and monetize it accordingly.

What separates many people from what they want and what they can realistically obtain, is what they ultimately do with their time. The essence of time is a very important factor when it pertains to wealth and needs to be looked at from many different perspectives. If you are reading this book and you are flat broke do you have free time that you are giving away to your TV Screen or Netflix?

If you are in a situation in which you are broke because you can't find a job, I want you to shift your mindset right now! If this is you, this means you have a lot of time that needs to be put to good use. So, if you believe that only someone else will compensate you for your time then you need to see value in your own time.

The amount of time that I see people waste is interesting to say the least. If you truly want to be successful and achieve all those big dreams and goals that you fantasize about, you need to be a master at time management. How much time are you spending reading, learning, or investing time into being a master in your niche that you want to be successful in?

With access to information easier to obtain than ever before, there is no excuse for sitting around and "waiting" for an opportunity. If you don't have any resources right now, what is the last book you read about earning income outside of a job? There are hundreds, probably thousands of books out here on ways to survive outside of a cubicle but ultimately, it's your responsibility to seek out that knowledge. If you want to be a successful entertainer, how much time and energy have you spent actually learning the business you want to be successful in? Out work the work and commit yourself to using your time to create your own opportunities.

When it comes to building wealth, time is crucial and is often overlooked. The correlation between wealth and TIME is twofold.

On the one hand, time and wealth are intertwined because if you truly want to be wealthy, what are you doing with your time? If you want to be wealthy, do you spend more time reading or watching TV? Do you spend more time at the mall or learning about what's trending in the stock market? Do you spend time on social media to bullshit around or do you spend time on social media to make money? Do you spend more time hanging out and partying or do you spend time trying to build a business to have real wealth? The answers to these questions will show you how to change your future immediately. What you spend your time and money on shows what you value, so what do your values consist of?

The other way that TIME and wealth are correlated, which is the most important point, is that time is the most important factor. It is the most important factor because when you study wealth, you learn that most wealth is accumulated over TIME through generations. Most of the people you see with real wealth, derives from previous generations and took TIME to build. Even Warren Buffet's children say they were not rich when they grew up, but over *time* Warren has been able to build a multi-billion-dollar empire known as Berkshire Hathaway. Now their father is a multi-billionaire but it took time and consistent efforts for him to build that empire.

Furthermore, time also plays an important role when trying to build wealth in the stock market. This is one of the main reasons why people don't invest is because they don't understand the essence of time. Too many people have a myopic view of life and are looking to get rich fast. This get rich quick mindset costs your family millions over generations.

Accordingly, it is important to note that we all have access to creating generational wealth. The great Dr. Boyce Watkins is the developer of the $5 a day investment plan. This plan shows that with only $5 a day and with TIME, ANYBODY can build wealth no matter what CURRENT financial state they are in. He always talks about having a 100 -year plan for your family and starting NOW to leave a legacy for future generations. Dr. Watkins has since become a great friend of mine and one of the main inspirations for this book. His teachings and brilliant ideas are light years ahead of anything you will see in mainstream media.

It is ludicrous for our children to have to start the wealth game from scratch with every generation. That is not black excellence. The same dialogue of "You better go get a job" or "go figure it out for yourself" is totally backwards. No, go *create* a job for your child and hire them. Then give them the proper tools to live a financially efficient life so that you can prepare them financially for the future. If you think that I am crazy for thinking this way, I want you to go out and look at almost every other community and study their family dynamic. Go into the Chinese stores, laundromats, or nail shops in your neighborhood, who is working there? If you want a job, will they hire you? Every other community has a culture of taking care of their own but we always think someone else's ice is colder not knowing our grass is green enough on our side of the fence.

I want you to really look at almost every other ethnic group and study the way they look at family business. Study the way that wealth and family are all tied together. Now look at how our community is, we

41

all live separate, work separate, and give our entire day labor to another community for them to build an empire. Then, when we are finally compensated for our hard-earned labor that same money is then extracted to another community to send their kids to college. Don't you think that the way we live our lives in the African-American community needs to be re-evaluated?

Again, the main point I want to stress in this book is the importance of long term thinking. You know the saying "TIME heals all wounds" - well I truly believe this and with the right amount of time almost anything can be accomplished.

Why TIME is worth more than money

Many people always say time is money, yes, it is, but TIME is actually worth more than money. If you lose money you have a chance to get it back, but when you lose time there's no chance you are getting that back. If you want to be great at something (which I know is the case because you are reading this book) you need to treat your time like you are the President of the United States and keep it precious. I waste NO TIME. That is how I am able to get things done. The time spent just to write these words that you are reading right now took a lot of sacrifice and carving out dedicated TIME to have the ability to share these words with you. Because it is important to me, it is worth my time sharing what I have learned with you.

I want to also personally thank you for taking the TIME to actually read this. See how important time is? Putting in that extra TIME to work on your dream will get you closer than spending your time looking for an emotional high. Once you treat your time like the asset that it is, this will open up a new mindset. You will see how much TIME you really have.

I always look at the case in which there is an older person with lots of money and a younger person with no money. If you are under 40 would you take a million dollars to be 75 years old? I hope that answer is NO.

If you are older and you have some money, would you give up your fortune to be 25 again? You may be surprised to learn that the answer to the first question is almost always no and the second one yes. Why is that? Because TIME IS WORTH MORE than money.

So, if you have no money, look at all the TIME you have to go out and do great things. If you are stuck at a dead end 9-5 job, when you get off work what are you doing with your time? Are you watching *Love and Hip Hop* or learning how to escape from your corporate position? After you put your kids to bed are you watching Netflix or reading a book on how to be successful and personal development to learn wealth building strategies? What we do with our time is everything. Still not convinced? Reflect back over your day. What does it reveal about what is important in your life?

Trading time for dollars

Another trap that many people fall into is trading time for dollars. The reason why we get so attached to that 9-5 is because we are trading time for dollars. The reason why I am writing this book is to tell you that there are alternative ways other than trading time for dollars. It starts with having a PRODUCER's mindset.

Think about what TIME you can spend producing something that can earn you money. For example, I am taking time to write this book which could translate to dollars at a later time. IF I only believed in an hourly rate for my time, I would never have had the courage to write this book and share my ideas with the world.

What can you produce? What can you spend time on now that can translate to dollars on your own terms? Then how can you rinse and repeat then create a system in which you are no longer trading time for dollars and earn a living on your own terms? That is the key to entrepreneurship which I will cover in the next chapter.

Once you start learning the essence of time when it comes to developing a system that works when you don't, you will start to experience the beauty of passive income. In this sense, the mind over money principle for time is that we should never let good productive time go to waste, EVER. Mind over money for time means that we spend time on entertainment and emotional highs AFTER we spend TIME on the things that matter first. I love spending time winding down to Netflix and chill, but that is normally after I have spent a long day putting in the time into producing things in my business that I know will have a positive impact on my future.

It's all about planting seeds. How many seeds are you planting? What are you doing right now that will impact the future to come? Everything that happens is a manifestation of an event that occurred in the past. Many people become shocked when a situation happens as if it just appeared out of thin air and isn't correlated with the past. "How did I get pregnant?" Did it come out of nowhere or is it because of an event that took place in the past? If you are currently in a financial rut what events took place in the past that could have caused this? I know for most of us what DIDN'T occur in the past was being taught financial intelligence. Because of this past misinformation, many of us have found ourselves in bad financial situations. This is why we can no longer use that as an excuse because now we know where the gap in information is and have to have a new mindset to leave for the future generations.

CHAPTER 6 – ENTREPRENEURSHIP

I hope that with each page you read about the mind over money principle, it starts to sink in deeper and deeper. Another big piece of this philosophy is the opportunities that exist in entrepreneurship . The topic of entrepreneurship is something that is very passionate for me because entrepreneurship has literally changed my life.

If you would have told me 5 or 10 years ago that I would be doing what I'm doing right now, I would have said that you were crazy. When you have your mind over your money, entrepreneurship comes as a central way to earn a living. Now this does not mean that you HAVE to be an entrepreneur or you have to have all of your income come from your own business, but it does mean that making your own money needs to be considered as a realistic option.

My Entrepreneurship Story

My journey as an entrepreneur has been one that I could probably write 2 books about. I gave you some brief background in Chapter 3 about my previous experience working in corporate America but now let me tell you about my transition into becoming a full-time entrepreneur.

Like I stated in Chapter 3, I was not happy working in corporate America and I knew that I had a deeper purpose in life, I just didn't know exactly what at the time. After getting fed up with corporate slavery, I finally decided to leave that situation and put my time and energy solely into building something on my own.

In hindsight, I see that this was not the most strategic move but I had my mind made up that I was tired of the corporate bullshit. I could have found another job, but I knew it would be a different theater but more than likely the same movie that had become a nightmare on Admiral Way with Freddy, Jason, and Michael Myers all after me. So, I decided to venture on my own and become "my own boss." Sounds good right?

I had no idea at the time how hard entrepreneurship really was. Entrepreneurship is one of the hardest things I have ever had to do in my life, no exaggeration, yet it is one of the most rewarding jobs. Again, back to time and how precious it is, the fact that I now have *full control* over my time and can do what I want on a daily basis is priceless. This is why I don't waste time; I can't afford to. Stepping off from your full-time job and thinking you are on vacation every day, is a sure way to guarantee yourself a spot right back on that plantation. No amount of money is worth being able to run my own schedule and put the time and energy into something I am truly passionate about and something I KNOW will benefit my family for generations.

Now you may be thinking again, "Ok Ryan, but how did you realistically do it?"

"How did you get to where you are now without going back to your 9-5 job?"

Well, the short answer to that is I had money saved up and money tied up in investments.

As soon as I started working at my previous financial institution, I immediately became an investor. These are the main funds that I had access to float me over without running back to a job. But more importantly, what I also did was spend countless time learning the craft. Entrepreneurship is not just about "being your own boss" or "having your own business." Entrepreneurship is a culture. I had to become a student of the game and get immersed in the culture.

I read countless books about business, listened to entrepreneurship podcasts, attended many digital live trainings and in person networking events, just to name a few things. I also built relationships with other successful entrepreneurs and got around them to pick their brains on how they overcame their journey. In any situation that you are in, I guarantee you there are many people out here who already experienced that same issue and can give you guidance. Your goal is to find them and try to get around them. If you want to jump into the entrepreneurship pool you can't be scared to get wet.

When you have your mind over your money, you recognize the countless opportunities that exist in being an entrepreneur, especially in the online space. It is ludicrous to think that the ONLY way to earn a living is to get a job. The deeper I get into entrepreneurship, the more I learn about so many opportunities that are out here. The cheap price of digital real estate out here is unprecedented and it is something that you **NEED TO KNOW**. The price of digital real estate today is like Malibu beach front property priced from 100 years ago or Manhattan real estate in the 18th century. The African-American community needs to be fully aware of the digital revolution and get on board with digital entrepreneurship or we will get left behind.

Believe it or not, there are people that you probably never heard of and could walk right past you that are making serious money from being an online entrepreneur. One person who stands out to me is an entrepreneur named Russell Brunson. Russell Brunson is the founder of Clickfunnels, a SAAS (software as a service) company that grew to 100 million in revenue in less than 3 years with no venture capital funding. To build a business that huge without Venture Capital funding is an amazing accomplishment. What was his secret? He has since written 2 best-selling books to give you insight on how he did it, but his main secret is that he builds profitable sales funnels on the front end, to change the way he acquires customers. Books, as I have discussed before, can provide you with blueprints that you can model for your own life.

Brunson's story, in particular, is interesting because he did not start out with any money but was determined to learn how to become an entrepreneur and learn how to make money online. These are the stories that we need to be studying , not just about how to get "put on" as an entertainer or worship a celebrity's Instagram to make money. Again, the people that I know with REAL money don't brag about cars, clothes, or jewelry; they are making hundreds of thousands of dollars a month from profitable sales funnels.

I can't stress enough the importance of having your mind over money when it comes to entrepreneurship. I encourage you to use this book as a launching pad to learn the many ways to make money as an entrepreneur. Please email me at info@ryanjmccrary.com and let me know about your progress. Please don't hesitate, I am looking forward to hearing from you.

Tax write offs

Another main reason why you want to consider entrepreneurship, is because of the tax benefits. Being a business owner opens up a world of tax breaks that you don't have access to being an employee. The tax write-offs and ways to use your business as leverage will put you in a new world of the way you live your life. This is why I truly believe that going forward, for the future of our community, our children need to be trained on entrepreneurship.

With the changing economy, and how technology has and will continue to replace jobs, we need to be PLANTING SEEDS NOW so our children will be able to survive. Being an entrepreneur gives you the skills to make money on your own and not be vulnerable to an employer.

I know that with the current political discourse there is a lot of talk about "how good the economy is" and "the unemployment rate is the lowest it's been since the 90s" which is true but for whom? Yes, the economy is good for me considering I am an investor and business owner, but what about the people who don't fall into that category? I have news for you; it's only going to get worse.

My prediction for the future of America and those who will economically survive is those who understand entrepreneurship, those who are producers, business owners, those who invest in stocks and bonds, and those who are land owners. It's not hard to see this reality in our everyday life. Even the jobs that are out here don't pay us what we deserve and with the high cost of living it seems like we are almost making less each year. Many companies don't pay those quarterly bonuses and raises like they used to, but the cost of living still dramatically increases every year. Even if you make over six figures, the living expenses you think you can afford often times, you may still find that you are living paycheck to paycheck and don't involve a serious and strategic wealth building strategy.

Now let me level with you and tell you the other side of entrepreneurship that many people don't tell you. ENTREPRENSHIP IS HARD AS HELL. While I do believe that everyone should at least look into entrepreneurship or at least invest in a business even if you have no intent to run one, if you do want to jump in this game is not for the weak. The rat race is not designed for you to escape so if you want to do this entrepreneur thing full time you better put on your seatbelt and get ready for this bumpy ride.

Be prepared to be constantly broke, putting your last into building your business, robbing Peter to pay Paul. Not being able to go out to that party because it would be more beneficial for you to go to this networking event. Staying in on a Friday night to read a book about how to grow a company. Entrepreneurship is about making sacrifices, tangible and intangible. Many people look at the high levels of success that those individuals achieve, but often miss the journey they went through to get them there. Mark Cuban said he didn't take a vacation for 7 straight years because he was building his business. Are you able to miss out on years' worth of vacations to build something great? Mark is now a billionaire so it is an easy debate on whether his sacrifice was worth it. Are you willing to make sacrifices for your dream?

I can say that it does seem to be "cooler" nowadays to be an entrepreneur, unlike ever before. It also opens up the door for many posers who are only "entrepreneurs" on social media, not real players in the game. Successful entrepreneur and media mogul Gary Vaynerchuk talks about this brilliantly and speaks from experience on what it truly means to be an entrepreneur. I follow his brand and what he teaches about the REAL side of entrepreneurship.

Entrepreneurship isn't about taking nice filtered pics on Instagram standing in front of a Mercedes Benz using hashtags about being an entrepreneur. Entrepreneurship is about WORK! Constant WORK. It's about building a system and learning how to grow a company. Make more than you spend, acquire customers, rinse and repeat. Sounds easy right? Easier said than done. Entrepreneurship is about putting things into the market even though you have no idea how things will turn out. Entrepreneurship is about staying up all hours of the night learning how to build out a new sales funnel.

I take some of the foolery personal because I am a true student of the game and not afraid to show it. I'm all in and not afraid to say that I don't know everything or at times I didn't know what the hell I was doing. I'm not afraid to say if a product launch I did failed or if I lose tons of money running the wrong advertising campaign. Entrepreneurship is not about a $99 network marking pyramid scheme where you have to sign up 3 others and then those 3 others get 3 more and you can build "residual income" and "become your own boss" and pay that monthly fee they call your "business overhead."

"Where else do you know that you can have you own business for just $39 a month?" You're right, you can't, that's why that is not a business. Being a real entrepreneur or business owner gives you equity in your own business. Real equity. You need to have an operating agreement that displays everyone who has a role in the company. You need to have a Federal EIN number and be registered with the state and local tax offices. Real entrepreneurs are the ones who I have come to admire and respect immensely.

So now that you are getting your mind over your money, you now are thinking about other ways to generate income for yourself and your family. The average millionaire has 7 streams of income. Now we are not

ONLY thinking about ways to make money from a job, we are also thinking about all the possibilities that exist in becoming an entrepreneur especially in the online space.

Some examples can be e-commerce, membership sites, affiliate marketing, online stores, online products, online services, selling an e-book, physical book, clothing line, or online course.

Again, the first thing you need to do is discover your passion and then find a way to monetize it. What are you passionate about? What would you enjoy doing every day that you would do for free? OK, once you have identified your passion, go out and starting finding ways to get paid for it.

CHAPTER 7 – RELATIONSHIPS AND MONEY

Another factor that could make or break your ability to gain true financial freedom is what personal relationships to choose to engage in. Now, I know someone will be reading this book and think that love and money should be totally separated and "who you love" has nothing to do with wealth, financial literacy, etc., but after you come down off your emotional high, I will say to you that they are so related it's not even an argument.

Any real financial analysis will tell you that who your partner is will make or break your financial situation, simple as that. Now, that does not mean that if you date or marry someone who is poorly educated on financial literacy or if they have NO money management skill your marriage will fail, no not at all! But it does mean that it will AFFECT the marriage , like it or not, right or wrong , so if you are having trouble overcoming financial hardships , it may be because of who you committed to. Now that doesn't mean to just flat out leave them, but you should at least recognize this and realize that they go hand in hand. If no matter how hard you try, you can't seem to overcome financial hurdles time and time again, it may be because of who you are in a relationship with and you need to try something new.

Money and relationship (not married)

Many people will argue that money has nothing to do with who you date or who you are in a relationship with if you are not legally married. That is true but only to an extent. Since marriage is a business and you do have to legally sign documents after getting married and all business owners know that when the contracts come into play, this is when it gets serious. But let's look at it from other perspectives.

Again, this book is about not looking at things from a traditional perspective. We just discussed a few chapters back the essence of time and how important TIME is when building wealth and financial literacy. So, if you are in a relationship with someone and you KNOW they are not even at least considering getting on board with financial intelligence, why waste TIME on someone who will give you a negative ROI?

Of course, people can change and introducing new ideas could bring real change but how many times do you hear the story about years of WASTED TIME for being in a relationship that could have been cut short from the beginning. What about the money you spend? Fellas, of course we want to spoil our lady, but are you throwing money at a dead situation that will not get you anywhere? I have spent lots of dollars showering women who I THOUGHT I could build with, but material items will not change a mentality.

How much TIME, and MONEY did you waste trying to build something that was unbuildable? If someone fooled you for years I want to offer my support, that is terrible, no one should go through that, but if you have seen this from the beginning and were trying to lie to yourself, once you have your mind over your money, you will have no TIME for BS. We are building empires and black excellence through generational wealth and have no time for people who will get in the way. We won't be able to save the entire community but we do have millions of people out here who see the future of our community through financial intelligence at the core of it. Seek out those individuals and build an empire with them.

Also, when dating just being around negative energy or energy that has no interest on making smart financial decisions or seeing all this finance stuff as "too serious" and "living day to day" "just happy to be here" with no real plans to truly thrive economically will take its toll on you. You could be the most ambitious person in the world, but just being in a relationship with someone who could care less about financial literacy can rub off on you indirectly. How bad do you want to get ahead? Are you willing to settle and be complacent or are you willing to achieve greatness by any means necessary? I'm not telling you at all to sacrifice all the not so perfect relationships that you encounter, but I do believe you should be at least THINKING about the fact that Money and relationships are vastly correlated and have it help your personal decisions and not have to be the victim of bad mistakes you've made in the past that have real financial outcomes.

Now let's look at marriage. The way that money is precedent in marriages is scary. Marriage is a business. Whether you like it or want to acknowledge it or not, marriage is a business decision. Being in a relationship is one thing and can affect your wealth accumulation if you let it, but legally marrying the wrong financial person is recipe for disaster. I will tell you that personally, I am not yet married. I do want to be married, but yes, I am speaking from a perspective of not being married. Now many people look at me being 30 and not married yet as if it's a bad thing or that I don't want to be married. Yes, I would love to currently be married, but I have not yet gotten to a place in my life that I have jumped the broom yet. I believe that I understood the relationship between marriage and money at a very young age which is why I haven't gotten married yet. What do you think?

With that being said, let's dig deeper into the correlation between money and marriage. Just looking at it from an objective view we can see that number one the divorce rate in America is 50%. So, don't you think that in something in which there is a 50/50 chance it will not work out that this is something you should think about deeply and make a very wise decision? You would be amazed at how many people would disagree with me.

Also, financial data shows that 70% of all wealth is lost during a divorce. I could name countless celebrities who you see the ex-wives took over half of their fortune just for making a bad marriage decision. Just because she had a nice body you wanted to spend the rest of your life with her. So, think about it, your retirement plan, all your stocks, bonds, businesses, and or property half gone just because you married the person who you THOUGHT you knew. All I am saying is choose carefully if you want to realistically get ahead and thrive financially.

This book is for people who realistically see building wealth as an option. Not the people who only TALK about "getting money" all the time and get motivated by an Instagram video. This is for the people who actually want to be able to provide resources to our community and truly want to turn their dreams into reality. Once you realize your dreams CAN become reality you will recognize who you chose as your spouse plays a big role in that.

The importance of money with other relationships

Now let's look at the relationship money plays with other relationships other than who you lay next to every night. Just became someone is your best friend doesn't mean you need to go into business with them and vice versa. The person you have legally incorporated a business with may not be your best buddy, but when it pertains to business and getting things done, they are great for the job.

"Your Network Is Your Net worth"

Have you ever heard the saying "Your Network Is Your Net Worth?" Well, I am a true believer in this philosophy. If your circle is 5 broke people just sitting around, best believe you will be the 6th. But if you have 5 BROKE people but all determined to do better (build something, etc.), you can truly build something great if you are focused on executing not just TALKING . Look at almost every financially successful person and I guarantee you that they have an amazing network . Your network is truly your net worth. How many people do you know that have access to resources that could benefit you? Whether it be capital or just access to a platform that you know will help boost your brand? How many people do you have in your rolodex that you can collaborate with or cross market with? That stuff matters . This is the reason many people feel the "white man's ice is colder" because of his access to many of these networks that have been built over generations.

If you are reading this and you have not yet built a real network of power players, that is ok, that is why I am writing this book. The #1 rule in networking is to offer something FIRST. This is something that premature aspirators often miss because they are too worried about something to GET from the person that is already established. No one owes you anything. Offer something of value FIRST. That number one thing may have to be money, and if you have the money and you KNOW this person will benefit your situation, pay it NOW! It will be well worth it.

If you are reading this and you don't have the budget to pay those thousands of dollars in consulting fees or training courses, think of other things of value you can offer. Again, if you are flat broke you probably have lots of time, so try to offer your TIME to that person you are trying to network with. If they are successful they will definitely see the value of time and may just put you in their office. If you are selling a product and you know that this person's influence can help you move units, give them the product for FREE and see if they like it, see if it brings value to their market place. You may even have some specialized skills that you may not see as value but the person may and in exchange they will give you mentoring. There are many ways to get around paying lots of money upfront , you just have to be willing to go do it. Again , things rarely happen overnight.

Being part of a community of people all committed to helping each other and are like-minded on goal setting, personal development, learning, etc., will give you the network you need to thrive economically. There are tons of communities out here online and offline, it's up to you to go out and seek them. They are definitely out here.

So, with the mind over money principle we now know that if someone says money has nothing to do with relationships, who you marry, who you hang out with, etc., run faster and faster into the opposite direction. Ok, let me relax, let's not run from them. Let's give them the CORRECT information that it DOES matter but being financially literate means that you recognize this and use it to your advantage.

One of the things that I do see that we need to correct is that many lawyers and legal analysts always want to be doom and gloom or only show you the ugly side of financial turmoil in marriage. We don't hear as many stories about the GREAT partnership and Economic Empires that are built and sustained through the beauty of marriage.

The reasons why many lawyers only discuss the bad divorces is because the big financial winner in divorce is the lawyers. Lawyers in this industry are making a killing so if the divorce rate decreases they are not making as much money! Aha! Again, it all comes back to money.

When you find that spouse that is on board with you on building an empire, greatness will occur. Knowing someone has your back and sees the importance of wealth building will give you the fuel to work harder and harder. In turn, you begin to internalize this drive and it changes how you see the world. Almost every great and highly successful individual had a spouse right there with them and would attribute much of their success to having that partner by their side.

Now knowing all of this and having your mind over your money, you know the importance of finding a soul mate who actually cares about all this stuff or even better trusts you to handle the financial decisions (i.e. you don't have to worry because he/she won't blow it all at the mall or max out the CREDIT card for retail therapy) and you see how you can truly build an empire. Do you know how much wealth is really out there? Don't get caught up on going to the "best restaurant" - find a way to own the restaurant. I want the stocks, the bonds, the 529 plans, the Trust Accounts, the many different retirement accounts. I want to own the crypto, the Bitcoin, Litecoin, Ethereum, ripple, etc. I want to own the block and have checks coming to me every month. I want to develop an estate plan to protect our wealth so it grows for generations.

When you are married if he or she has debt YOU have debt, if she is in a bad place financially YALL are in a bad place financially. Marriage is a partnership and business decision that needs to done using financially intelligent lenses. Make sure you are investing in a partner that will be an asset not a liability.

CHAPTER 8 – BEING RICH VS. BEING WEALTHY

A few chapters ago, I briefly mentioned that there is a big difference between being rich and being wealthy; now we will go more in depth about this very important concept. I think that a lot of the smoke and mirrors about what it means to have money is a misconception of this core principle.

I grew up like many other young black boys in America. I was born in 1987 and am the definition of a 90's kid. As a kid, I wanted to be "rich and famous." My first aspiration was to be an NBA player and get paid millions of dollars. I grew up wanting to be a basketball player and a rapper. I am not going off of some data about a demographic on a statistic chart, I *was* that kid. There are so many of our young boys that really buy into that dream of becoming a sports player or rapper. This does not mean that it is not possible, we just need to look at it from a realistic perspective.

Why do so many of our black boys want this so bad? I truly believe it comes down to American culture of "wanting to have money" and seeing people we can "relate to" appearing "successful" and "having money." This is again why we *have to* change the dynamic on how much media plays a role in how we live our lives, especially the youth. Why don't we aspire to be doctors or lawyers the same way we aspire to be sports players and rappers? Lawyers and doctors make really good money too.

Now let me say this now before we go any further, this is NOT in any way a criticism on any athletes, rappers, singers, actors, actresses, or any celebrities that are successful. I commend any celebrity that has overcome hard times and gets paid to do what they love. Another mistake many people make from the outside when they look at successful people and think they "got lucky" and NEVER look at what it took for them to get there. Most celebrities and successful people work VERY HARD and work at a level the average person won't be willing to do in order to achieve that high level of success.

Now also looking at it from a realistic perspective, we CAN'T have millions of children and many adults for that matter, who think the only way to "get rich" or have lots of money is to play sports, act, or become a musical entertainer (rapper, singer, etc.). The numbers just don't add up. There are only a few hundred spots annually to meet the demand of being a celebrity and almost everyone except a few will be left out.

I have great news for those people (sssshhh don't be too loud) you can still have a high income or high levels of success without dribbling a basketball or going into a recording studio. Yes, it may take some time and won't happen overnight after signing a contract, but it is something that CAN be achieved. But you have to have your mind over your money.

I say this all to say that as children and even as adults we rarely ever learn the difference between being RICH and being WEALTHY. Most athletes are rich and fewer are wealthy but the owners of the team ARE WEALTHY. Many rappers are rich (less are rich than you think) but the WEALTHY are those who OWN the record labels and are the executives. Not the ones you see on IG with the cars, cash, etc. The ones with the REAL POWER OWN the label, not get SIGNED to the label. Let me break down the concrete differences between being rich and being wealthy.

Rich	Wealthy
High Income	Have sustainable income
Money usually dies when they die	Own assets
Only have cash	Money that lasts over generations
High expenses	Their money works for them
Still have to work for their money	Passive income exceeds their expenses

We need to be aspiring to be wealthy not just to be rich. When you are rich, many a time you still have to WORK to receive that nice income. If you are a celebrity and you make over a million dollars a YEAR but still have to constantly WORK to get that money, go on promo tours, put out albums, movies, etc. that is great, but what happens when you don't get that next BIG movie deal or what happens if you don't want to do any more movies or put any more songs or albums out? You will have a hard time trying to make those millions of dollars a year and keep up with that lifestyle. When you are wealthy, your money works for you. You don't work for your money. When you own property, your property usually appreciates without your having to do anything, due to how the real estate market increases.

When you own stocks, you may receive dividends without

WORKING to do it, and business ownership also gives you the ability to earn without actually working in the business. Wouldn't you want to earn lots of money without having to actually WORK for it?

Now when I discuss these principles with people, some say "Ryan, that all sounds nice, but I like to actually get UP and WORK for it. I can't just sit back and collect, I like to go out and get mine." And I agreed with this sentiment whole heartedly. But I said, ok, but for how long? How long are you going to have to go out and get it? What if God forbid you were confined to a bed for long period of time and couldn't GO OUT and get it or what about when you grow old, don't you want some type of residual income ? I believe that once you have a hold on receiving passive income, it gives you the ability to GO OUT and get whatever you want, but the key is that you DON'T HAVE TO! When you are wealthy, you DON'T HAVE to do anything to make money. However, when you are rich, you still HAVE to do something to keep up with that fortune. Which would you prefer?

Another misconception is that wealth has everything to do with how much CASH you have which is false as well. You can have lots of wealth but very little CASH and have lots of CASH but no wealth. Just because you have lots of CASH doesn't necessarily mean you are doing well financially. You can take a credit card and go get $50,000 worth of Cash and take a picture and put it on Instagram. Now people will think WOW he's rich or wealthy because he has $50,000 worth of cash but they don't know that person is now $50,000 in the hole in debt. Perception is not the same as reality. We need to understand these principles and not get caught up in an illusion.

Net Worth

In the last chapter, I talked about how your network is your net worth which I believe to be VERY TRUE, but many people don't even know what net worth really means. Net worth is your ASSETS MINUS YOUR LIABILITES. An asset is something that you own that is worth something (the value of your home, the value of your investments – stocks, bonds, mutual funds, retirement accounts, college funds, royalties, or stake in a business or corporation). Your liabilities are any debt or anything that you owe (e.g. an existing balance on your mortgage, credit card debt, car loans, student loans, or any other form of debt or loan in which you OWE something). What you OWN MINUS what you OWE is how you determine your net worth. This then, is an indicator of your financial well-being.

Net worth is NOT about how much money you MAKE a year, or any fancy degree or job title that you may have. Many people think that because they went to school and now have a nice job that means that they have a high NET WORTH. This is not the case. We need to be educated about this so that we will know how to truly build wealth and obtain real financial intelligence.

This is important because the main goal should be wealth accumulation, real wealth, generational wealth, but we have to KNOW what wealth IS. Again, another misconception is that the car you drive means you have WEALTH. A car is not WEALTH. Yes, a car can show up on the asset side of the balance sheet if you have no car loan, but a car typically does not appreciate and does not hold its value. Assets put more money into your pocket, liabilities send money out. Which one do you have more of? What the wealthy do is they get their ASSETS to pay for their expenses or liabilities. They don't buy liabilities and give the crumbs let over to purchase assets. This is the foundation of getting a wealthy mindset and recognizing the truth on how to make American capitalism work in your favor.

The applies perfectly to our mind over money principle for many reasons. First, when you have your mind over your money, you know that there is a difference between being rich and being wealthy. You understand what net worth really is, and don't get caught up in the nonsense. You also understand that building wealth takes time.

One of my idols that I have come to personally know very well is Kenny Gamble. Kenny Gamble is a Grammy Award winning musician and song writer who has worked with some of the biggest and most legendary names from the 1960's and 1970's.

What's so interesting about Mr. Gamble is that when he received his millions of dollars in royalty checks, the first thing he did was go to individuals who could teach him how to make his money work for him. He didn't get caught up in the flash and material items, he focused on how to build true wealth, an economic empire, and not HAVE to depend on record sales or a label for financial security. This all goes back to the foundational fundamental wealth building principles I have been discussing in this book. When you are rich, you still have to depend on getting that big new movie deal, or you have to focus on putting out that next BIG HIT, but when you are wealthy you know that your assets will appreciate and make you money, whether your career is doing well or not .

Needless to say, Mr. Gamble has built an economic empire with a large portfolio of real estate and control over a number of schools. All while giving back, being humble, and never FLASHING any money. His story needs to be studied more and used as the blueprint for black excellence.

When you recognize the real difference between being rich and being wealthy, you will realize that YOU can go out and make it happen for yourself, you don't have to depend on anyone. As long as you are incorporating learning, reading, knowledge, asset accumulation, and building relationships as a foundation, there is NO reason why you can't make it happen. The REAL money is from quarterly profit distributions and business acquisitions, not likes, followers, and views on social media. Now go out and forget trying to be rich, let's become wealthy and give back to the community while doing it.

CHAPTER 9 – OWNERSHIP IS THE REAL AMERICAN DREAM

What is the American Dream? The definition of being materially successful is the image that most Americans want to align with achieving "The American Dream." But, what is the American Dream? The American Dream is supposed to be getting a good formal education, and then going to a good college. After you graduate from college, you are supposed to get a good paying job, buy a single house in the suburbs, with a white picket fence, and have 2.5 kids. That is when we know we made it, right? Wrong and here's why.

We must start by asking: Who defines this dream? Who developed and made *this* the American Dream? The American Dream that is mostly talked about is some made up fantasy that never seemed real in the world I grew up in.

I grew up in a single parent household because of the untimely passing of my father when I was 5 years old. He suffered a severe heart attack at the age of 46, which forced my mother to raise 2 children on her own with help from my aunt and grandmother. Without my family, I do not know where I would be right now. We must prepare our children with the REAL knowledge that will give them the opportunity to be competitive in society.

Anybody with a brain should know that the American Dream is subjective and means a lot more to different people. My definition of the American Dream is EQUITY. Equity is Ownership! The people who make the rules and get ahead in America, are the people who own and control resources. Simple as that. This is a fundamental fact that many people don't think about enough.

What you own and control will determine almost everything about what you will get in our society. When applying all of this to the mind over money principle, we now know that we do not define how well a person is doing financially by how much money they make, but by what they own and control.

Bragging about how much money you make and having that define your entire financial well-being, is like still playing sports in the little league. When you look at what assets you own, you are now playing with the Pros.

Again, I want to reiterate, the people who get ahead in America are the people who own businesses, the people who own real estate, and the people who own stocks and bonds. NOT the people solely focused on how high their income is. Having a high income is great, but owning assets is better. This also leads back to the being rich vs. being wealthy principle.

Looking at our culture and our value system, I often see equity at the last end of the conversation. We have been duped into thinking that high salaries, fancy cars, and lavish spending defines what it means to "have money." Yes, that's a great way to "look rich" but all truly wealthy individuals know the first rule of getting money is to hang on to your money. There are countless numbers of millionaires you probably see on a daily basis who you would never know have so much money. This book is to give you the foresight to know how to build TRUE WEALTH and TRUE EMPIRES, not just to "look like" one. We need to shift the mindset to owning assets.

When it comes to how you make a living, are you getting a paycheck or do you own the company? So, for those that brag about their high salary and look down on those who don't earn as much as them, I say the real power is the person who owns the company. I want to own the company, even if the company doesn't look like much at the present time, there is so much power in equity.

Think about all the Billion-Dollar companies that were started with a dream and were passed up by so many. Think about Amazon, Apple, Microsoft, etc., even Blockbuster had the chance to buy Netflix in the year 2000! When's the last time you rented a movie from Blockbuster?

Most of these large conglomerate companies were ideas that were shared to previous employers and were passed on. A company would rather pay you that salary than to give you ownership, why is that? Equity is power.

So, I would encourage you to go out and OWN SOMETHING. You don't have to become a millionaire overnight (it would be pretty hard to do anyway), but you can go out and OWN SOMTHING. I am willing to bet that almost anybody reading this book has the ability to own something! Whether it be $5 in an investment portfolio or a simple domain name that you OWN, that can turn into a digital real estate empire. If you don't at least have the mindset you will never achieve great things.

Again, this book is about a mindset shift and knowing the CORRECT information on where the *real* money is. The real money is owning and controlling assets, simple as that.

Now let's revisit a person's potential living situation. Do you pay someone to live in their place or do you OWN the property? The fortune is in the equity. So, bragging about an amazing looking pad, is again still low on the totem pole. If you OWN the property, you have the gold. You make the rules, you can choose who you want to or not to live in the place. You can rent it out using Air BnB and get passive income, just to name a quick example. Ownership is the real American Dream. Think about the people who make the decisions in our society, they OWN some type of resources.

There's nothing stopping you from owning your own resources. That is to have the Real American Dream. Once you realize and actually *act* on this principle, you will realize that anything you want is obtainable. Real power is in ownership.

The third most important way that people get ahead in America, are people who OWN stocks and bonds. Not people who just work at the company, people who OWN shares in the company. When you are an employee with no equity, you have no say on who they hire, board members, etc. But when you are a shareholder, most shares come with voting rights. You have a SAY on who you want to run the company that you have a STAKE in it, and guess what? You don't have to do any labor! That is passive income my friend, that is how you become a true boss!

If I didn't know any better I would still be in the same position and have the same mindset, but now I know what true power is. I know that ownership is what *real* bosses have, not just "looking like money. "

One of the best, if not *the* best, resource for taking a deeper dive is to study the work of the legendary Dr. Claud Anderson. He has written two life changing books, *PowerNomics* and *Black Labor White Wealth*. Dr. Anderson gives his readers the blueprint on how owning and controlling assets opens up the door to the fruits of American society, and most of us don't even understand this enough to even use it to our benefit. But, that is no excuse.

It's bad enough that we don't engage in these activities and don't develop a true wealth building strategy, but most of us don't even know about or even understand what the real problem is. If you have a bunch of cash but don't OWN anything , again you are still a rookie in this wealth building game. It is okay to be rookie, nothing wrong with that at all, but don't brag and boast about it. This is why big corporations are laughing at us when we line up for Jordan's, but won't line up at the NYSE. They KNOW that there is no power in having material items.

We live in an era where perception and reality try to get intertwined too much. The part that social media played to redefine our society is one that has never been done before and we will only know the results later on down the line when we go back and study history.

All I am saying is don't get caught up in the hype. Make sure you have your mind over your money and take care of business first. That's all I'm saying. The steady way to win this uphill battle with having a strong financial life, is to own and acquire assets. Simple as that. This should be on your mind daily. Redefine the way you think, redefine the way you look at the world and viewing someone as "successful." When you think about that successful person or if you get bent out of shape for seeing someone "winning" and you should be "winning" too, go back and think what do they own?

When you own and control resources, you make decisions. Walk into the bank with OWNERSHIP in a truly profitable business or a nice size real estate portfolio. Talk to your local politician about that thing you WANT DONE and back it up with ownership of assets and real numbers of what YOU OWN. Watch how your conversations and network will change. Ownership is everything.

This is why African-Americans are always left behind when it comes to politics. We don't own anything collectively, so we have no base to stand on. Sure, we have some politicians that are doing well, which we love and commend. But we don't have a real collective economic base that owns any resources.

Dr. Anderson talks about how we have neighborhoods not communities. Communities can thrive and survive by themselves and can function off each other. We need to control the economy in our own community.

If you watch the show *Shark Tank*, which I do, you always see how equity is a very important factor. Why is that? Because OWNERSHIP is the Real American Dream.

Now, since you have your mind over your money, we no longer SOLEY view "living the American Dream" by the job you have, the car you drive, or the house you live in. We view it by OWNERSHIP . What do you own? If you don't own anything now, go out and own something. It is much easier to OWN than to get caught up just earning and spending everything you get. I truly believe in ownership over income. Income is good but can fade or not or leave you vulnerable , but when you own assets, they will appreciate . It puts you into a whole other category and you will be right at the table with the real movers and shakers who control the society in which we live.

CHAPTER 10 – GENERATIONAL WEALTH

Now we will discuss probably the most important part of this book. Since we now understand the importance of equity, and how it shapes our realities in America, we will now discuss how to protect your assets and have them pass on from generation to generation.

Generational wealth is something that is a very important concept and must be looked at with the correct information. I love how I am slowly but surely starting to see conversations around generational wealth for African-Americans on a mainstream level.

If you look at the most recent album *444* by Jay Z, you will see how Jay brilliantly describes the importance of generational wealth and that the real money is in assets. Jay Z, the one who taught us all how to stunt and do it big, is talking about the importance of financial literacy? Why? Because this is the movement and the wave of the future. I commend Jay for shedding light on this and using his platform to define true black excellence.

The days of holding stacks of cash to your ear and doing MTV cribs in a rented house are days of the past. Remember MTV cribs? I used to love that show as a kid and had no idea at the time that most of that was all smoke and mirrors.

This is why I have written this book, because I KNOW we have to have our mind over our money. And we must have a blueprint for doing so—one that is accessible to the masses and explained in a way so that all readers can walk away with pragmatic information.

Another reason why I feel like I am well-suited and in a good position to deliver this message is because I have been in those buildings. What buildings are you talking about, Ryan? I'm talking about those trillion-dollar investment firms, sat with million-dollar investment bankers, those big companies, and multi-billion-dollar insurance companies. I've been in board rooms with multi-million-dollar clients and high-level Principals.

I'm not talking about the head of a junior high or high school. I'm talking about investment Principals that head multi-trillion-dollar corporations. I've seen the lack of color in those rooms and their uninterest to change that. And frankly I'm not mad at them. The people who built these companies did not build them for "everybody" to be a part of them. Don't get mad when you don't get included, build your own corporation.

I just wanted to give you the background to let you know that generational wealth is not something I "heard about" or just "read a lot of books" about. I've seen it up close and personal, how it walks, talks, and looks at the world. I also see the gap in what separates the haves from the have nots, and a lack of information and knowledge is at the forefront of it.

What generational wealth really is

Before we move on let's take some time to just state what generational wealth really is. Generational wealth is when a family has an economic base which consists of a large sum of capital. It could be a trust fund or a multi-million-dollar business. It could be equity in a fortune 500 company or a large real estate portfolio. Generational wealth can consist of many different assets but it is usually a large sum of capital built up over time. Wealth is an accumulation process, it is not an over- night get rich quick scheme.

One of the simplest ways to pass something on to your heirs without being "rich" is having the proper life insurance. Life insurance can leave something to your family even if you didn't have much to give while you were alive. Master P has previously stated before that his business got started from a life insurance policy and he has since turned that into hundreds of millions of dollars. This fits in perfectly with the mind over money mindset because many people don't THINK about having life insurance or how that plays a part in the wealth building journey.

When you have your mind over your money, you start thinking about life insurance, and then you will find out that life insurance premiums are probably less than your cable bill. Is cable more important than leaving wealth for your family?

Go out and search and I guarantee that a million dollar life insurance policy is less than what you pay in a car note, especially if you are under 40. Again, this is not to go tit for tat or say one or the other, all I'm saying is realistically you can have both. When I tell this to some of my clients they say that they had no idea about this or didn't look at it from this perspective. They then thank me for providing them INFORMTION they did not know.

It's all about information folks. But it's also your personal responsibility to ACT on the information. We need to take action. This book is about *taking action* and I want to give you all the tools to have a financially successful life.

Sharing Financial Information

Another point that is important when it pertains to collectively getting ahead, is to share this financial knowledge when you have it. There are many tokens in America or people in high places that when they get there don't want to share this important information to people. This holds us back. I personally love sharing information that I know will be helpful to others; it keeps me going. When you have a good heart, if you hear some very valuable information, you have no choice but to go back and share it with the masses so we can all be successful. I truly believe in collaboration over competition.

Now this may be a lot of information to consume, especially if the whole wealth building mindset is all new to you. But let me bring it back down practically and remind you that wealth, or generational wealth for that matter, all comes back to family. Your family dynamic is everything. Even if you can't get the WORLD on board with financial literacy and wealth building, just try to get your IMMEDIATE FAMILY on board. Start gathering and just TALKING about these concepts. TALK about developing a family business, talk about the stock market and how millions are being left on the table in the long run. Once you start TALKING about it, it will put you in the proper position to then ACT on it and make it part of your family rituals.

Many families were never introduced to these principles so give them this information and remind them to outdate any thinking of the past.

Prior to integration, there were tons of black businesses and blacks did own and control their own communities. They had no choice. We always talk about how we "achieved freedom" after the Civil Rights Movement, but in hindsight, we see we won a battle that put us behind in the war. The war of ownership and control of resources. We gave up our assets to be "accepted" only to have in return to obtain a seat at SOMEONE else's table.

Let's turn the tide and build our own FOOD chains, so they can have that seat at OUR table. Of course, they are stories of Black Wall Street, Rosewood, FL, etc. about Black WEALTH that was stolen and never recouped. This then leads to a conversation about Reparations and what should or should not be done. Again, this is not a political book, but if you care to know my position on the reparations subject, I do believe African-Americans are owed reparations 100%.

So, I find it offensive when people, especially black people say "we have never had wealth." I look puzzled and say well when are you talking about? We had ownership and assets 100 years ago with Black Wall Street. We owned our own neighborhoods in the late 19th century, right after the Civil War.

What about the days in Africa before slavery? Mansa Musa was the richest person in the history of the world long before Bill Gates and Jeff Bezos. Knowing the REAL HISTORY is also a big part of building wealth for the future. We have to know about this excellence to recreate it and make it a reality in our lives.

How you view money – Personal Responsibility

Another big part of generational wealth is how YOU view money and personal accountability. The way people view money and what I see in society is a big part of why I wrote this book. Many of us view money from a miniscule perspective. Money should be used as A TOOL to give us the choice or ability to do what we want. It should not just be the end result. In earlier chapters, I explained my complex view of money. I explained how I believe money, especially in America is ALMOST everything, because it determines where you will live, if and what you eat, what school you are able to send your children to, and access to health and medical benefits. I also believe that you can be the richest person in the world and still be miserable.

I truly believe in Maslow's hierarchy of needs and believe that once your basic needs are met (i.e. food, shelter, clothing) the only time you should stress over money is when you need to get your message out to the world. Again, financial freedom is not about having a lot of money, it is about how free you are to do what you want and if loving what you do for a living exceeds the amount you need to live.

Many of us are so worried about "getting money" that we never take the time to actually STUDY money. Learning how money really works and learning from experts and people who understand the truth. I hope this book is a launching pad for you to look at things from a different perspective. Again, this book is not about telling you what to do, but for you to think about all of this and understand that there is a science to realistically building wealth.

It is also about personal accountability. Many people try to blame the past or other individuals for the state they are in. That can definitely leave hard effects and impact your life, absolutely, but at some point, you need to think about what you did or did not do to determine where you are. Look at the glass half full and say no matter what goes on from now on, I want to make the commitment to improving my financial health. Once personal accountability is taken, you can only go up from there.

This ALL comes back to mindset. If you don't think you can build wealth you never will. But once you KNOW you can, and you see the countless resources out here, you know this is a long-term play, and your destiny lies in your own hands.

The mind over money's long-term play is generational wealth. Many people don't even know what generational wealth is and what it looks like to even start the process to build it. You are not in that category. The beauty of the internet opens up the doors to all the information in the world, we just have to be committed to soaking it all up. It's about leaving a legacy that will survive 4 generations after you. Be that pioneer that went against the norm and left a legacy. This is your way to immortality.

CHAPTER 11 - THE NEXT GENERATION TO SAVE THE BABIES

Another big part of generational wealth and preparing the next generation is having little to no DEBT. It is bad enough having to start over every generation with NO assets and NO wealth but it's worse to have your heirs start in the red. Many of us actually start out in the NEGATIVE which makes it even harder to build wealth!

It's hard enough when a family member passes on with no life insurance, but it's even more difficult when they pass on debt too and leave their family in a bad place financially. Let's do our best to eradicate debt. Debt is financial slavery. Yes, that new car "looks nice", and those red bottoms at the mall "look good," but when you walk into that bank or that VC and want to start making real money to fund that business idea or to buy that house, those flashy items hold no weight on the balance sheet. The bank doesn't care how fly you think you are or who you kick it with, that doesn't matter. Let's have our mind over our money and take care of business first.

Protecting your assets

As important as it is to *know* this information and take action on it, it is equally as important to put the proper documentation in place to protect your wealth. The four main concepts when it comes to wealth protection and preservation of assets are life insurance (which we talked about), trust accounts, having a will, and proper estate planning.

Life insurance

Like we discussed in the previous chapter, life insurance is extremely important. It is a clear-cut way to make sure you leave money to your family when you die, because trust and behold we all will die at some point. It's only fair to make sure your heirs are left with something. Is also important because these premiums are not as much as we sometimes think. Let's make this a priority and take care of business first.

Trust accounts

Trust accounts are legal entities that have a fiduciary responsibility to protect assets. I would encourage you to sign up for one of my courses at www.makingfinancialliteracycool.com so you can fully understand how trust accounts work and how to use them to your advantage.

The importance of having a will

The importance of having a will in place is something that is also often overlooked. I have spoken with many clients, most of them of the baby boomer generation, who never thought to develop a will. This is extremely important especially when you have wealth and many assets. A will specifically says who, what, and where will happen to your assets when you are deceased. Who you want your money to go to and who can act on it. This is one of the keys to protecting your wealth! You've probably seen news stories where family empires are diminished because someone did not have a will in place upon the death of a wealthy relative.

In order to develop a will, all you need to do is to contact an estate attorney and have them draft up a will document for you. It is not as hard as you may think but will save your family's wealth. If you don't have one yet, especially if you are over 50, go out and get one now!

Estate planning

Like wills, trusts and life insurance all play into properly engaging in estate planning. Estate planning is having the legal documents in place on what will happen to your ESTATE once you pass on. Your estate is all of your assets. Once you've built up your assets, it is imperative that you contact a good estate attorney and plan your estate. You want to be able to avoid the "death tax" and probate court. You want to make all of the necessary and legal ramifications so you are able to pass wealth down to future generations smoothly. This is the final piece to solidifying your legacy.

CHAPTER 12 - IMMEDIATE STEPS YOU CAN TAKE RIGHT NOW TO LIVE A BETTER FINANCIAL LIFE

12 Immediate Steps you can take to start living a better financial life NOW

Now that you've read through almost all of this book and understand the mind over money principle, I hope you are now ready to take action and actually put this into effect. I sincerely wish the best for you in whatever your aspirations are.

The reality is that everyone SAYS that they want to be financially free, but only a small percentage of these people actually take action to make this a reality. I want to do everything in my capability to make sure you are one of the individuals to do what it takes to succeed.

Below, I have laid out 12 concepts I want you to take action on IMMEDIATELY. These 12 items will propel you to earn the financial freedom and success that you deserve.

1) Start an Acorns Account

The investment apps that currently exist today have made it possible for almost anyone to be able to invest. For a minimum of $5 you can instantly become an equity shareholder. Acorns is an app that invests the spare change from debit or credit card purchases and puts the spare money in an investment portfolio.

You also have the ability to just invest as often as you want or even have it automatically go in to build up compound interest. This is a great way just to get the ball rolling even if you think that you don't have the budget to invest.

2) Setting short term and long term financial goals

Setting short term and long term financial goals is vitally important to achieve the financial success you want to pursue.

Write it down or keep it in a Word document. Write down where you would like to be in the short term (1-2 years) and then write down your long-term goals (where you see yourself in 5-10 years).

For example, I may write down:

- How much revenue I want in my business
- How much I want my investment portfolio to be worth
- What I want my career goals to be
- Where do I want to be in 2 years or 5 years

These are just some examples you can use to help you develop a short term and long-term plan.

3) Open a brokerage account

This is also something that is very easy and doesn't require a lot of money if you are just starting out. I must say again that this is NO

MEANS giving investment advice, performance, stock tips, or any recommendations. I am just stating an option that gives you the ability to start really building wealth. Once it is on paper it is real.

Many brokerage firms have a minimum requirement of about $50 or $100 to start and this gives you the ability to purchase stocks. This is just one way to develop equity with extra money you don't spend on "going out as much."

4) **Connect, via social media or other platforms, with mentors or people who are currently where you want to be.**

This is something that has vastly benefited me and it did not exist in the past. In the past, we didn't have so much accessibility to successful people at the snap of a finger. Now you can literally find anyone you want via social media or technology. Even if the people in your circle see no value in changing, start getting close to one of these mentors. This will save you years of trial and error.

5) **Consider purchasing a duplex**

As we discussed, the ownership of real estate is an important part of financial literacy and building wealth. Consider and look into an option for owning a duplex, it can provide you passive consistent income or at minimum have you live for free or substantially lower than if you didn't own one.

You also have to ability to build up equity and have it appreciate.

6) **Attend Offline Networking events**

This is important because with the current digital landscape, it is easy to get comfortable with just networking online or ONLY attending webinars. Being online is great, but there's nothing like actually networking in person and building real live relationships with other people. This will put you in the position to be around like-minded individuals and to share resources that will help you get to where you want to be.

7) Start Your Own Business

We thoroughly discussed the importance of business ownership and I just want to reiterate that important point. Business ownership is one-third of the wealth building puzzle. When I first started my business, I had no clue what I was doing but I was determined to figure it out.

Starting my own business has been one of the best decisions I have made in my life and I don't regret it one bit. Of course, it is challenging and not cut out for the weak, but it is an option that just might change your life forever and make you a millionaire along the way.

8) Invest in getting a financial advisor

Since I have worked in and gained expertise in the finance industry, I have seen behind the scenes all of the hidden fees and other things advisors use to take advantage of clients. I usually say that a lot of the stuff financial advisors provide you with, you can do yourself and save a ton of money when you learn the information. Yet, there is still value in hiring a professional.

Hiring someone who is a professional in finance can be the bridge you need to meet your financial goals and he/she could have a great impact on your life. There are advisors out here that truly want to see you get ahead financially and can provide that one on one licensed advice that you may need to help get you to the finish line.

9) Get into digital marketing

Online sales and marketing, and just selling online products has literally changed my life. The money that exists in the digital economy is unprecedented and I think you have an opportunity to get a slice of the pie.

Start learning the science of digital marketing and how to earn an income in the digital space. You will see just how life changing it can be. The fact that I can be anywhere and still make money, motivates me even more and more every time a new sale comes in.

10) Carve out time at least once a week to evaluate your finances

A big reason why we get left behind financially is because we never set aside dedicated TIME to actually look at our budgets and make necessary adjustments along the way. Budgeting is crucial. Many times, we get so wrapped up in our expenses and think that "paying these bills" is the only way without ever siting down and detaching to actually figure out what is a necessary and what is leisure.

Getting serious about your priorities will make you realistically be able to build on it and replace old habits with financially healthy new ones.

11) Make a consistent effort to learn and understand what is going on in the world from a financial perspective

Almost every day I watch at least a little bit of CNBC just so I can get a glimpse of what's going on in the financial world. I would encourage you to do the same. That does not mean you have to watch Squawk Box or Mad Money every night, but it does mean you pay attention to what is going on. You can also pay attention to your local news when they talk about the stock market or put different stock ticker symbols on your iPhone watchlist. Staying in tune with the financial market is important and could give you the opportunity to get in on some Initial Public Offerings just because you knew about it.

12) Just do something!

The main point in this entire book is to DO SOMETHING! Throughout this book, we covered many different financial concepts and many different schools of thought on what you maybe should or should not do, but the main point is that you must do something!

If you read this book and get highly inspired but TAKE NO ACTION, then the time that you invested reading it is lost. Remember, time is a valuable resource.

I want you to truly put your mind over your money and go out and take care of business. The world is your oyster and your financial freedom is just one action step away from changing your life. At the beginning of this book, you may have thought that you didn't know enough about finances or building wealth, well now you have the blueprint and now you KNOW how to put your mind over your money. You now have the tools to go out and do it; you have no more excuses to hold you back, so go out and do it. And once you do, never look back unless it is to pull someone up with you.

RM

ABOUT THE AUTHOR

Ryan McCrary is a serial entrepreneur and former licensed securities agent. He received a Bachelor of Arts degree in Sociology from Temple University in 2011. After receiving his Bachelors degree, Ryan worked at Prudential Financial. He worked directly with annuities and then transitioned to a role as an investment professional with The Vanguard Group.

After over 5 years of experience in the finance industry, he decided to leave corporate America in order to deal with some of the economic issues within the African-American community. He is currently the owner and CEO of McCrary Financial Solutions, LLC, a digital consulting company whose mission is to provide economic solutions for the African-American community.

He is also an investor and recently opened TheMcCraryFinancialSchool.com, an online financial literacy institution designed to start a trend of financial intelligence and academic excellence.

Made in the USA
Lexington, KY
06 June 2018